The ⬚⬚⬚ olos

CON⬚⬚

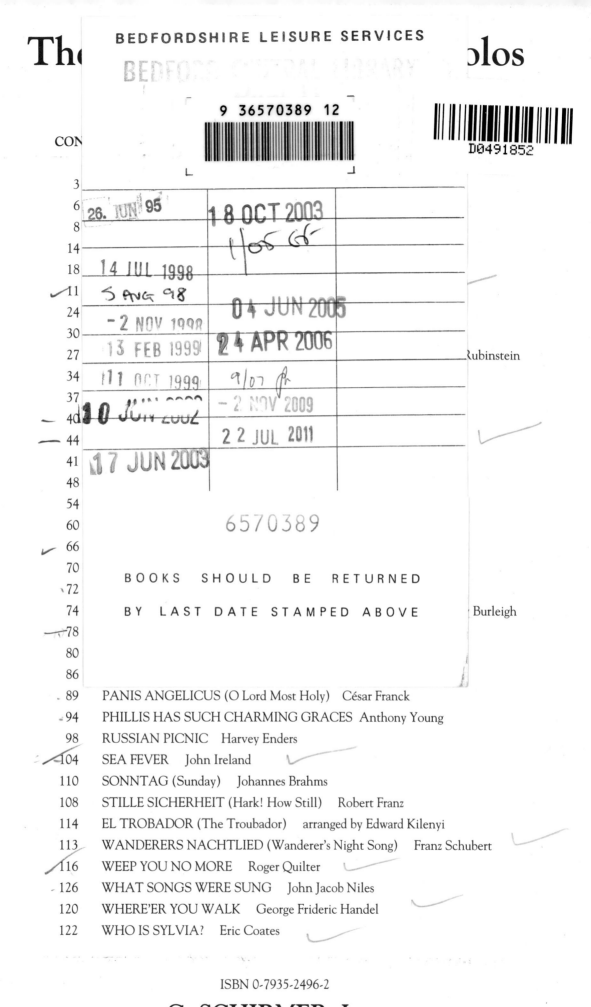

ISBN 0-7935-2496-2

G. SCHIRMER, Inc.

Distributed by
Hal Leonard Publishing Corporation
7777 West Bluemound Road P.O. Box 13819 Milwaukee, WI 53213

7.95

PREFACE

The widespread acceptance by teachers and students of "The First Book Series" for Soprano, Mezzo-Soprano/Alto, Tenor, Baritone/Bass has prompted the development of a Part II addition for each voice type. After discussions with numerous voice teachers, the key suggestion expressed many times was that there is a need for "more of the same" type of literature at exactly the same level.

The volumes in Part II follow many of the same concepts which are covered in the Preface of the original volumes, including a comprehensive selection of between 34 and 37 songs from the Baroque through the 20th Century. The selections range from easy to moderate difficulty for both singer and accompanist.

In response to many requests, we have included more sacred songs, and have added two Christmas solos in each volume. The recommendation for more humorous songs for each voice was honored as well.

Even though these books have a heavy concentration of English and American songs, we have also expanded the number of Italian, German, and French offerings. For those using the English singing translations, we have tried to find the translations that are most singable, and in several cases have reworked the texts.

Part II can easily stand alone as a first book for a beginning high school, college, or adult student. Because of the varied contents, Part II can also be successfully used in combination with the first volume of the series for an individual singer. This will give many choices of vocal literature, allowing for individual differences in student personality, maturity, and musical development.

Hal Leonard Publishing (distributor of G. Schirmer) and Richard Walters, supervising editor, have been most generous in allowing the initial objective for this series to be expanded more fully through publishing these companion volumes. We hope this new set of books will provide yet another interesting and exciting new source of repertoire for both the teacher and student.

Joan Frey Boytim
September, 1993

About the Compiler...

Since 1968, Joan Frey Boytim has owned and operated a full-time voice studio in Carlisle, Pennsylvania, where she has specialized in developing a serious and comprehensive curriculum and approach to teaching and coaching adolescent and community adult students. Her teaching experience has also included music and choral instruction at the junior high and senior high levels, and voice instruction at the college level. She is the author of a widely used bibliography, *Solo Vocal Repertoire for Young Singers* (a publication of NATS), and, as a nationally recognized expert on teaching beginning vocal study, has been featured in many speaking engagements and presentations on the subject.

ADIEU
(Farewell)

Charles Grandmougin
translation by Marion Farquhar

Gabriel Fauré

Com - me tout meurt vi - te, la ro - se Dé - clo - se,
All things die so quick - ly, the flow - er In show - er,

Et les frais man-teaux di - a - prés Des prés; Les longs sou-pirs, les
And the glow-ing rose that the spring Will bring; Long drawn-out sighs, the

bien - ai - mé - es, Fu - mé - es!
love we cher - ish, Will per - ish!

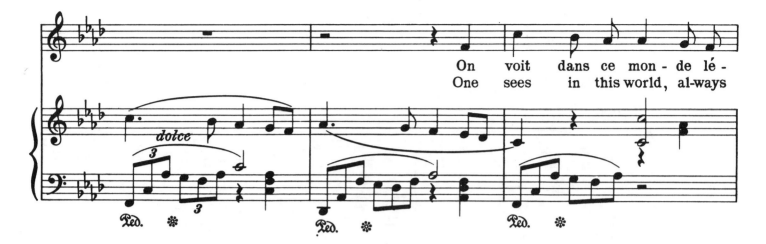

On voit dans ce mon-de lé-
One sees in this world, al-ways

ger, Chan - ger, Plus vi - te que les flots des grè-ves, Nos
light, In flight More swift than tides' in - con-stant stream-ing, Our

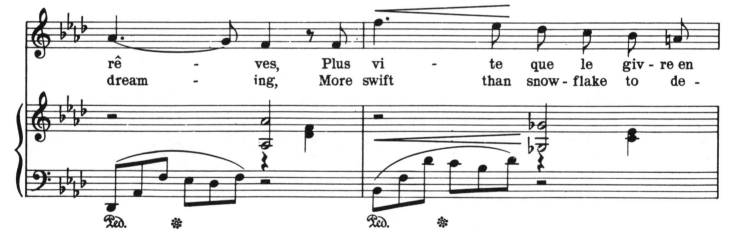

rê - ves, Plus vi - te que le giv - re en
dream - ing, More swift than snow-flake to de -

fleurs, Nos cœurs!_____ A
part, The heart!_____ With

vous l'on se croy-ait fi - dè - le, Cru-el - le,
you, one nev-er thought to leave you, De-ceive you,

Mais hé-las! les plus longs a - mours Sont courts! Et je dis en quit-tant vos
But it seems, long-est loves, a - las! Soon pass! And I say, from your beau-ty

cresc.

char-mes, Sans lar - mes, Presqu'au mo-ment de mon a - veu, A -
turn-ing, Un-yearn-ing, Al-most when vow-ing I'll be true, A -

dolce   *pp*

pp sempre

dieu!_____
dieu!_____

AN DIE GELIEBTE

(To the Beloved)

J. L. Stoll

Ludwig van Beethoven

Composed in December 1811.

AVE MARIA
(Father in Heaven)

English version by
Jacques Ahrem

Camille Saint-Saëns

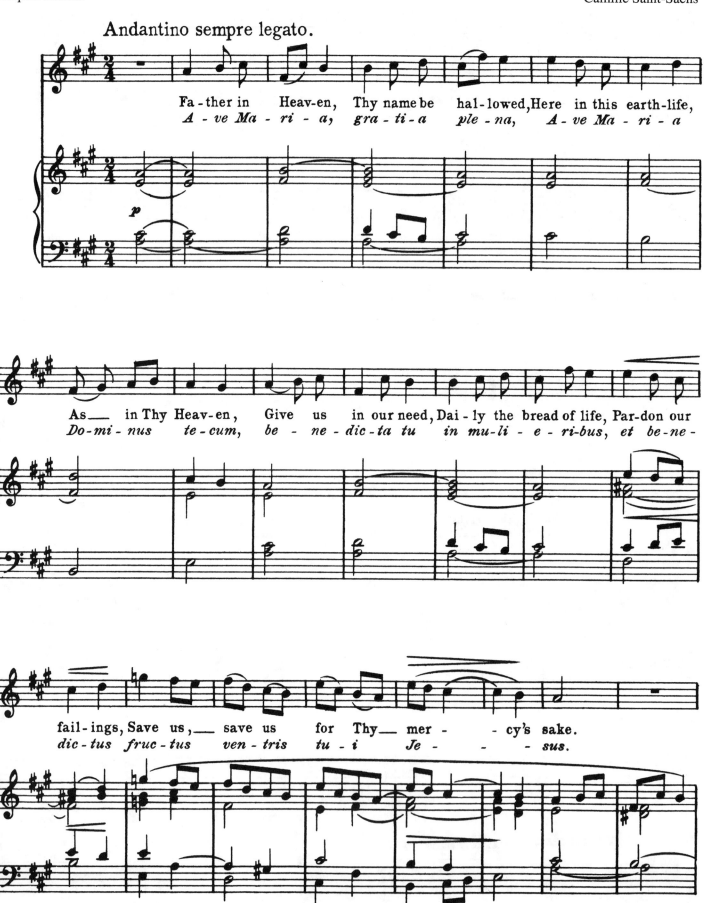

9

dolce.

us: Guard Thou and   guide us,   Till in Thy   king - dom,
træ.   *O - ra pro   no - bis,   O - ra pro   no - bis*

Prais - es for - ev - er,   Prais - es   ev - er - more we   sing____
nunc et in   ho - ra,   et in   ho - ra   mor - tis   nos -

dolcissimo.

____ to Thee,   Hear our__ pray'r, O__ Sav - ior,
- - træ.   O - - ra pro__ no - bis,

dolcissimo.

Let 'Thy mer - cy   be on us. _____
O - - ra pro no - bis. _____

rit.

THE CLOTHS OF HEAVEN

William Butler Yeats

Thomas Dunhill

night and light and the half light, I would spread the

cloths un-der your feet:

But I, be-ing poor, have on - ly my

dreams; I have

spread my dreams un-der your feet; Tread soft - ly,

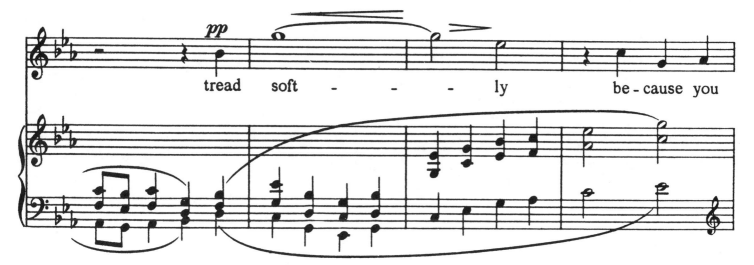

tread soft - - - ly be-cause you

tread_____ on my dreams._____

THE BIRTHDAY OF A KING

text by the composer

W. H. Neidlinger

15

sky was bright with a ho - ly light, O'er the place where Je - sus

lay: Al - le - lu - ia! O how the an - gels sang, Al - le-

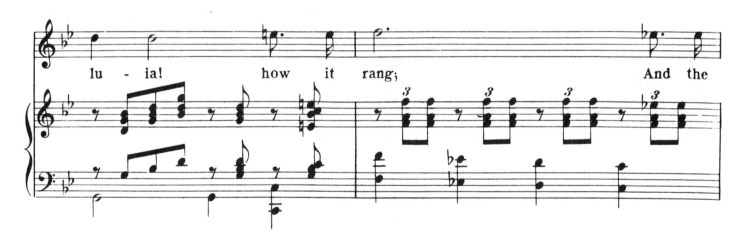

lu - ia! how it rang; And the

sky was bright with a ho - ly light, 'Twas the

birth-day of a King.

'Twas a

hum - ble birth-place, but oh! how much God gave to us that

day, From the man - ger bed, what a path has led What a

per - fect ho - ly way: Al - le - lu - ia! O how the

an - gels sang, Al - le - lu - ia! how it rang; And the

sky was bright with a ho - ly light, 'Twas the

birth - day of a King.

BONJOUR, SUZON!

(Good-Morning, Sue!)

Alfred de Musset
translation by Theodore Baker

Léo Delibes

tel que tu me vois,_____ D'un grand voy - age en I - ta -
gain, as you may see,_____ From It - a - ly and far a -

li - e. Du pa - ra - dis j'ai fait le tour,_____
way,___ dear! I've trav - ell'd Par - a - dise all through,_____

J'ai fait des vers, j'ai fait l'a - mour,_____
I have made love and vers - es, too,_____

un poco riten.

J'ai fait des vers, j'ai fait l'a - mour. Mais que t'im -
I have made love, and vers - es, too! But why should

por - te, mais que t'im - por - te? Je pas - se
you care? but why should you care? I'm pass - ing

de - vant ta mai - son, je pas - se de - vant ta mai - son,
by your door to - day, I'm pass - ing by your door to - day,

Ou - vre ta por - te, ou - vre ta por - te!____
So let me in, I pray, so let me in, I pray!____

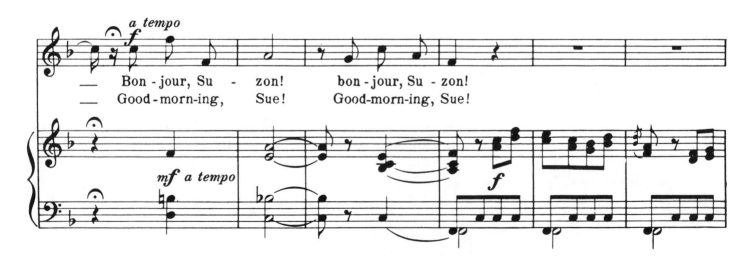

__ Bon - jour, Su - zon! bon - jour, Su - zon!
__ Good - morn - ing, Sue! Good - morn - ing, Sue!

UN DOUX LIEN

(Tender Ties)

Victor Wilder
translation by Theodore Baker

Alfred Delbruck

Un doux li-en nous en-la-çait tous deux,
Be-tween us twain were wo-ven ten--der ties,

Ton bras au mien s'é-tait ri-vé; _____ Quand, tout à coup, j'ouvris les
Thy soul in mine blend-ed her stream, _____ When all at once I oped mine

yeux: _____ J'a-vais rê-vé! _____
eyes: _____ 'Twas all a dream! _____

Ce tendre a - veu que j'im - plo - rais de toi, Ta lèvre
The sweet a - vow - al I im - plor'd of thee, Thy lips

en - fin l'a - vait trou - vé, Ton âme
had found: so might it seem, Thy heart

é - tait à moi! J'a - vais rê -
be - long'd to me: 'Twas all a

vé, J'a - vais rê - vé!
dream! 'Twas all a dream!

DU BIST WIE EINE BLUME

(Thou'rt like unto a flower)

Heinrich Heine

Anton Rubinstein

a) *Translation by Natalia Macfarren*
b) *Translation by L. L. Scaife*

Printed in the USA by G. Schirmer, Inc.

those gold-en tres - ses My fold - ed hands to lay,_____
ob ich die Hän - de auf's Haupt dir le - gen sollt',_____
though I must lay then My hand up - on thy brow,_____

Pray-ing that Heav'n may pre-serve__ thee So fair, so pure__ al - way,_____
be - tend, dass Gott dich er - hal - te so rein und schön__ und hold,_____
Pray-ing that God may pre-serve__ thee As pure, and fair__ as now,_____

___ Pray-ing that Heav'n may pre-serve thee, So fair, so
___ *be - tend, dass Gott dich er - hal - te so rein und*
___ Pray-ing that God may pre-serve thee As pure and

p
pure al - way,
schön und hold,
fair, as now,
p
Pray - ing that Heav'n may pre - serve thee,
be - tend dass Gott dich er - hal - te,
Pray - ing that God may pre - serve thee,
p
Ossia
rit.
So fair and love-ly, and pure al - way.
so rein und schön, so schön und hold.
So fair, so pure al - way.
so rein, und schön und hold.
As pure, and fair, as now.
pp
p
ppp

DOWN BY THE SALLY GARDENS

William Butler Yeats

Irish air
"The Maids of Mourne Shore"
arranged by Herbert Hughes

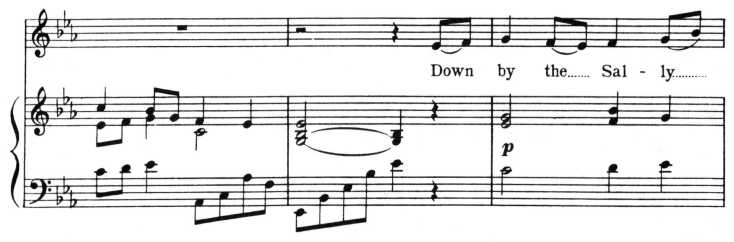

passed the.... Sal - ly gar - dens With lit - tle snow-white

feet. She bid me.... take love ea - - sy, As the

leaves grow on...... the..... tree, But............... I be-ing young and....

fool - ish With her did... not a - gree.

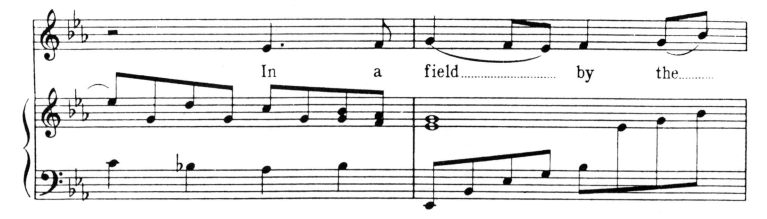

In a field_____ by the_____

riv - er My___ love and I did stand, And_____

on my_____ lean - ing shoul - - der She_____

placed her_____ snow - white hand; She

bid me take life ea - sy As the grass grows on the weirs, But I was young and fool - ish And now am full of tears.

EVERY DAY IS LADIES' DAY WITH ME

from *The Red Mill*

Henry Blossom

Victor Herbert

I should like, with-out un-due re - it - er - a - tion of the e - go, To ex-
It's a frightfull thing to think of all the hearts that I have broken, Al - tho'

plain, how ve - ry hard I find it is to make my pay go 'Round a-
each one fell in love with me with - out the slight - est to - ken, That my

mong my vul-gar cre-dit-ors I'm fear-ful-ly in debt, For I al - ways have af - ford-ed an-y-
fa - tal gift of beau-ty had in-flamed her lit-tle heart, But I found that some small fa-vor al-ways

Printed in the USA by G. Schirmer, Inc.

thing that I could get! But I must say I've en-joyed the best of
seemed to ease the smart. A po-si-tion for a cous-in or a

what there is in life; I've been luck-y in my love af-fairs I've
loan to dear pa-pa; Just a dain-ty dia-mond neck-lace or a

ne-ver had a wife! I can sum-mon lit-tle int'-rest in the
pret-ty mo-tor car. But I don't be-grudge the col-lar-ets and

dry af-fairs of state, And the bus'-ness-men who call on me are
neck-la-ces or pearls, All the mon-ey that I ev-er saved is

cold-ly left to wait! For ev-e-ry day is la-dies' day with
what I've spent on girls! For ev-e-ry day is la-dies' day with

FAME'S AN ECHO

from *Comus*

John Milton

Thomas Arne

Fame's an E - cho, Pratt - ling dou - ble,

An emp - ty ai - ry glitt' - ring Bub - ble

L.H.

A breath can swell, ___ a breath can sink it, The

Printed in the USA by G. Schirmer, Inc.

wise not worth_ their keep - ing think it

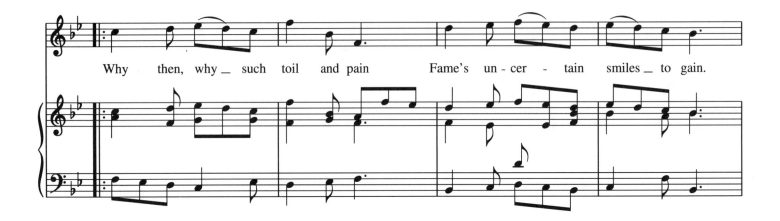

Why then, why_ such toil and pain Fame's un - cer - tain smiles_ to gain.

Like her sis - ter For - tune blind

To the best she's oft un - kind,

And __ the worst her fa - vour find,

And __ the worst her fa - vour find,

Adagio

And the worst ___ her fa - vour find.

f

FORGET ME NOT

translation by J. Troutbeck

from the *Schemelli Gesangbuch*

J.S. Bach

IN DER FREMDE

(In a Foreign Land)

Joseph, Freiherr von Eichendorff

Robert Schumann

mehr.
I.

Wie bald, ach wie bald kommt die
And soon shall I slum - ber in

stil - le Zeit, da ru - he ich
calm re - pose, With those still so

auch,
dear,

da ru - he ich
With those still so

auch,
dear!

und ü - ber mir rauscht die
And murm' - ring leaves of the

schö - ne ___ Wald ein - sam - keit, ___ die
fo - rest, shall whis - per my woes, ___ The

schö - ne Wald ein - sam - keit, und
leaves shall whis - per my woes; A -

Kei - ner kennt mich mehr hier! und
las! none know me here! A -

Kei - ner kennt mich mehr hier!
las! none know me here!

DAS FISCHERMÄDCHEN

(The Fishermaiden)

Heinrich Heine
translation by Theodore Baker

Franz Schubert

Poco Allegro.

PIANO.

Thou love-ly Fish-er-maid - en, Steer now thy boat to
Du schö-nes Fischer- mäd- chen, trei - be den Kahn an's

land, —
Land; —

Come to me and sit — be - side me, We'll
komm zu mir und se-tze dich nie - der, wir

whis-per hand in hand, Come to me and sit — be - side me, We'll
ko - sen, Hand in Hand, komm zu mir und se-tze dich nie - der, wir

Printed in the USA by G. Schirmer, Inc.

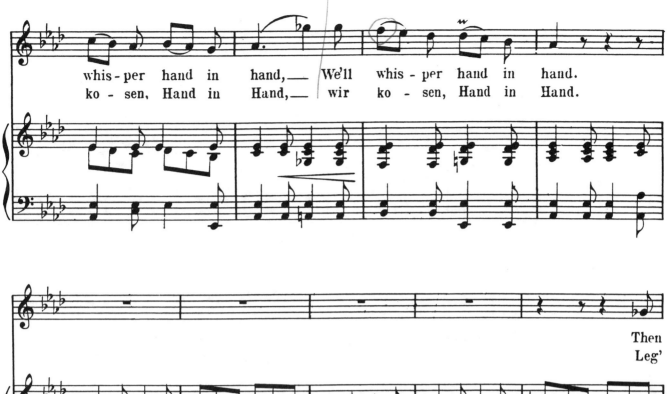

whis - per hand in hand,___ We'll whis - per hand in hand.
ko - sen, Hand in Hand,___ wir ko - sen, Hand in Hand.

Then
Leg'

dim.

lay thy head on my bo - som, Fear naught, but trust thou in me,___
an mein Herz___ dein Köpf - chen und fürch - te dich nicht zu sehr;___

For thou dost trust___ all fear - less,
ver - trau'st du dich___ doch sorg - los

Dai - ly the storm-y sea, For thou dost trust all fear - less,
täg-lich dem wil - den Meer, ver - trau'st du dich doch sorg - los

Dai - ly the storm-y sea, _____ Dai - ly the storm-y sea.
täg-lich dem wil - den Meer, _____ täg-lich dem wil - den Meer!

My
Mein

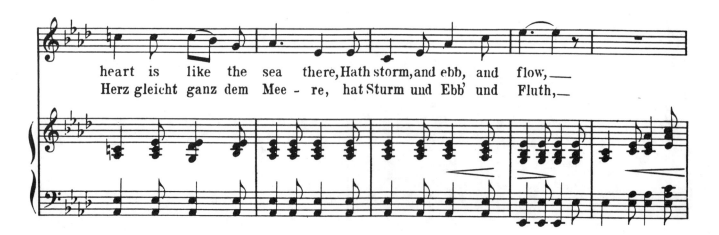

heart is like the sea there, Hath storm, and ebb, and flow, _____
Herz gleicht ganz dem Mee - re, hat Sturm und Ebb' und Fluth, _____

And many a pearl may be there, With-in— the depths be-
und man-che schö-ne Per-le in sei-ner Tie-fe

low, And many a pearl may be there, With-in— the depths be-
ruht, und man-che schö-ne Per-le in sei-ner Tie-fe

low,— With-in— the depths be-low.—
ruht,— in sei-ner Tie-fe ruht.—

dim.

INCLINE THINE EAR

Isaiah 55:3,1

Ernest Charles

soul shall live,_____ hear_____ and thy soul shall

live._____ In - cline thine ear, in - cline thine

ear, Hear_____ and thy soul shall live._____

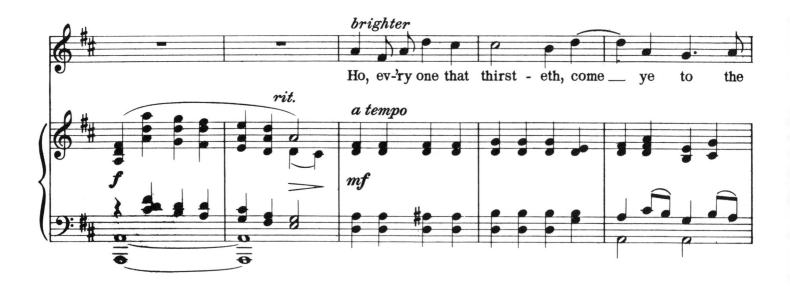

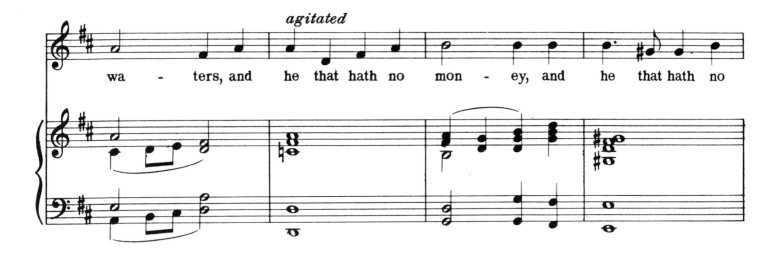

agitated

wa - ters, and he that hath no mon - ey, and he that hath no

mon - ey, and he that hath no mon - ey, come ye, buy, and eat.

As at first

In - cline, in - cline thine ear and come un - to

rall.

mp

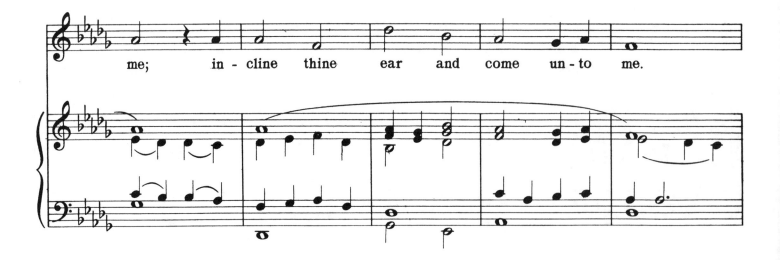

me; in - cline thine ear and come un - to me.

Hear and thy soul shall live,_____ hear_____ and thy

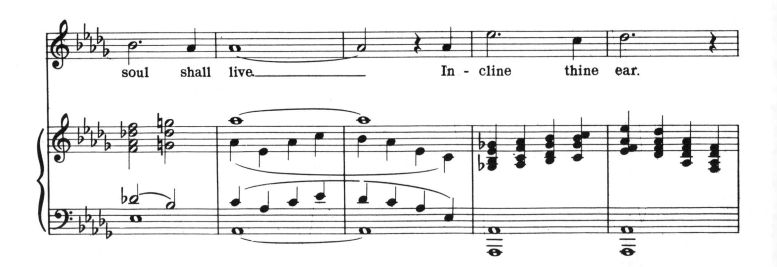

soul shall live._____ In - cline thine ear.

Come un-to me and thy soul, thy soul shall live.

Come un - to me and thy

soul shall live.

IT WAS A LOVER AND HIS LASS

William Shakespeare

Eric Coates

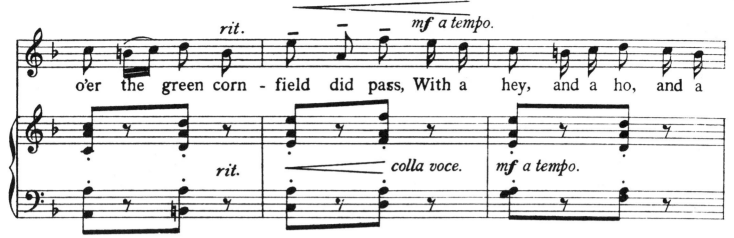

o'er the green corn-field did pass, With a hey, and a ho, and a

hey.... non-ny-no, non-ny-no, _____ In the spring time, the

on-ly pret-ty ring time, When birds do sing, when birds do sing, hey

ding a ding a ding; Sweet lov-ers love the spring. _____

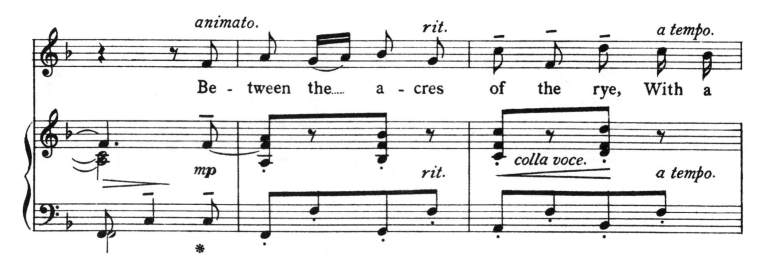

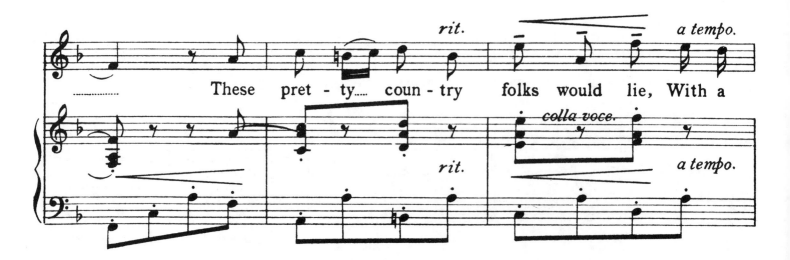

hey, and a ho, and a hey... non-ny-no, non-ny - no,...............

In the spring time, the on - ly pret - ty ring time,

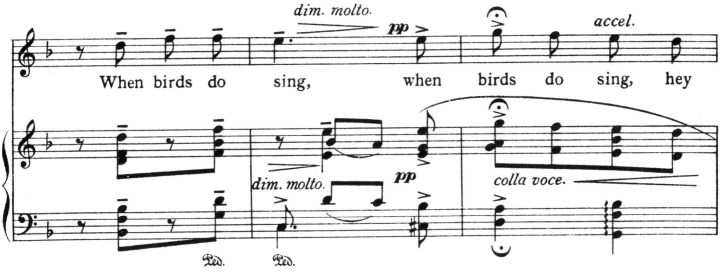

When birds do sing, when birds do sing, hey

ding a ding a ding; Sweet lov-ers love the spring.

57

And there-fore...... take the pres-ent time, With a

hey, and a ho, and a hey......non-ny-no, non-ny - no, ... For

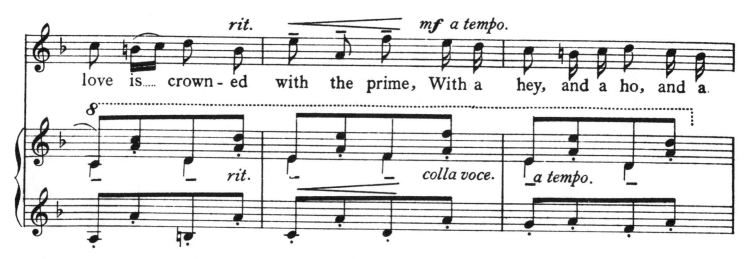

love is...... crown-ed with the prime, With a hey, and a ho, and a.

A KINGDOM BY THE SEA

Edgar Allan Poe

Arthur Somervell

It was ma-ny and ma-ny a year a-go, In a king-dom by.... the

sea, That a- maid-en then lived whom you may know By the

name of An - na - bel Lee. And this maid - en she lived with no

o - ther thought Than to love and be loved by me.

p

I was a child, and

she was a child, In this king - dom by the sea, But we

62

loved with a love that was more than love, _____ I and my An - na - bel

Lee, _____ With a love that the wing - ed ser - aphs in Heaven

Co - vet - ed her ___ and me. _____ And

Poco meno mosso.

this was the rea - son that, long ___ a - go, In this king - dom by ___ the sea, _____ A

wind blew out of a cloud, Chil_ling my beau_ti_ful An_na_bel Lee;

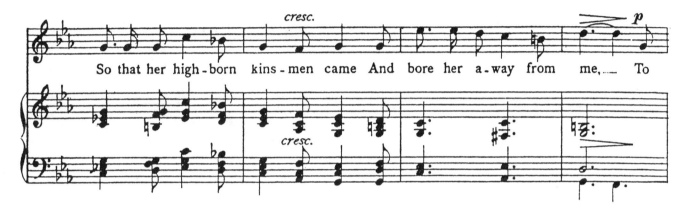

So that her high-born kins-men came And bore her a-way from me,___ To

shut her up in a se-pul-chre, In this king-dom by___ the sea,— My

beau_ti_ful An_na_bel Lee, My beau_ti_ful An_na_bel Lee.

But the

Tempo I^{mo}

moon ne_ver beams with-out bring_ing me dreams Of the beau-ti-ful An-na-bel

Lee;.............. And the stars ne_ver rise but I feel the bright eyes Of the

beau-ti-ful An-na-bel Lee. And so all the night-tide I lie

down by the side Of my dar - ling, my dar - ling, my life and my bride, In her

se - pul - chre there by the sea,___ In her tomb___ by the sound - ing

Alternative finish.

sea._____

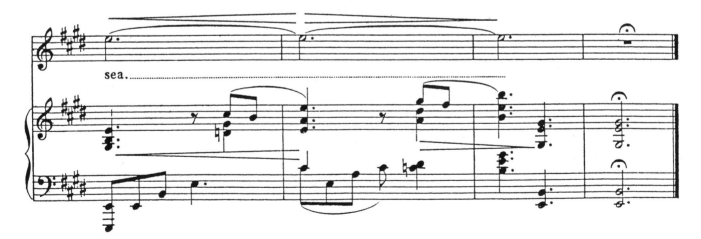

sea._____

LINDEN LEA

W. Barnes

Ralph Vaughan Williams

whis - tle o - ver - head, And wa - ter's bub - bling in its bed; And there for
whis - sle au - ver - head, An' wa - ter's bub - blen in its bed; An' there vor

me, The ap - ple tree Do lean down low in Lin - den Lea.
me, The ap - ple tree Do lean down low in Lin - den Lea.

colla voce

When leaves, that late - ly were a -
When leaves, that lëate - ly were a -

rit.

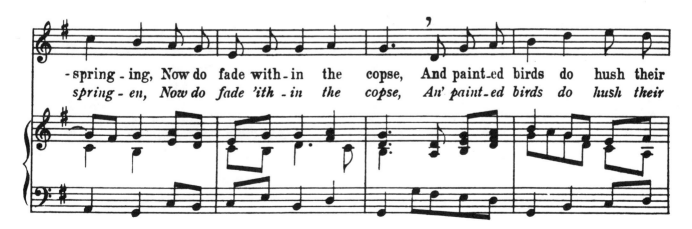

-spring - ing, Now do fade with - in the copse, And paint - ed birds do hush their
spring - en, Now do fade 'ith - in the copse, An' paint - ed birds do hush their

singing, Up up‿on the tim‿ber tops; And brown leaved fruit's a‿turn‿ing
zing‿en, Up up‿on the tim‿ber tops; An' brown leaved fruit's a‿turn‿ing

red, In cloud‿less sun‿shine o‿ver‿head, With fruit for me, the ap‿ple
red, In cloud‿less zun‿sheen au‿ver‿head, Wi' fruit vor me, the ap‿ple

tree Do lean down low in Lin‿den Lea.
tree Do lean down low in Lin‿den Lea.

colla voce.

mp

Animato. *f*

Let o‿ther folk make mo‿ney fas‿ter; In the
Let o‿ther vo'k meäke mo‿ney vas‿ter, In the

rit.

f

LOVE QUICKLY IS PALL'D

composed for a production of *Timon of Athens*

Shadwell, after Shakespeare

Henry Purcell

Love quick - ly is pall'd, tho' with

la - bour 'tis gain'd; Wine nev - er does cloy, no, nev - er does

cloy, tho' with ease, __ with ease 'tis ob - tain'd.

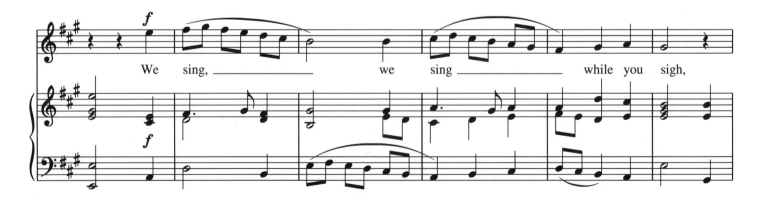

We sing, _____ we sing _____ while you sigh,

we laugh,____ we laugh,__ we laugh,_____

laugh while you weep;   Love robs you of

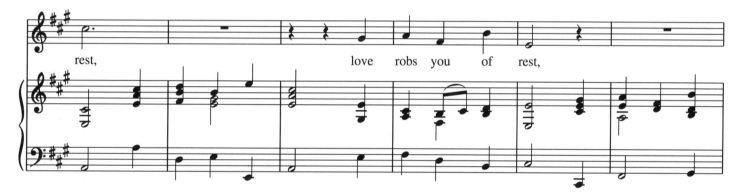

rest,   love robs you of rest,

Wine lulls____ us, lulls____ us, lulls____ us, lulls____ us, lulls us a-

sleep.

MY LOVELY CELIA

text by the composer

George Monro

My love - ly _ Ce - lia, heav'n - ly _ fair, As li - lies _

sweet, as soft _____ as _ air; No more _ then tor - ment _ me,

but _____ be - kind, And with _____ thy _ love _ ease my trou - bled

Printed in the USA by G. Schirmer, Inc.

NOBODY KNOWS THE TROUBLE I'VE SEEN

Spiritual,
arranged by Harry Burleigh

times I'm up some - times I'm down. Oh   yes,

Lord!   Some - times I'm al - mos'   to de groun';

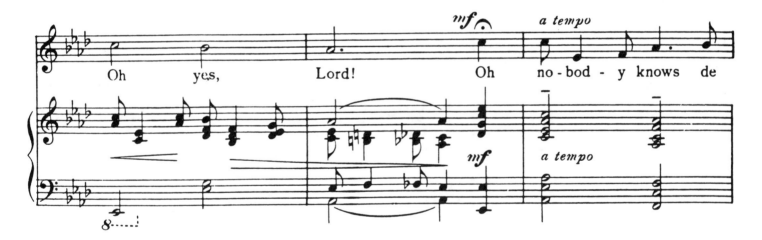

Oh   yes,   Lord!   Oh   no - bod - y knows de

troub - le I've seen,   No - bod - y knows but   Je - sus,

No-bod-y knows de troub-le I've seen, Glo-ry hal-le-

lu - jah! If you get there be - fore I do,

Oh yes, Lord! Tell all-a-my friends I'm

com-ing too, Oh yes, Lord! Oh

no - bod - y knows de troub - le I've seen, No - bod - y knows but

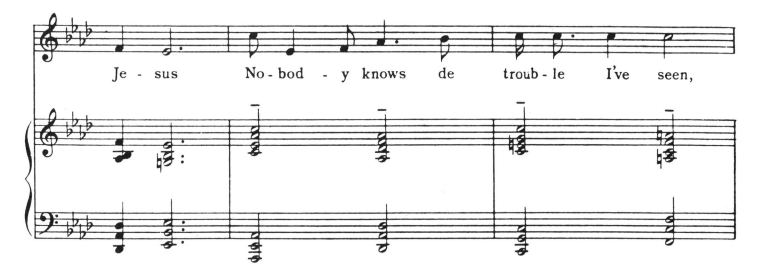

Je - sus No - bod - y knows de troub - le I've seen,

Glo - ry hal - le - lu - jah!

O COME, O COME, MY DEAREST

from *Fall of Phaeton*

Pritchard

Thomas Arne

Printed in the USA by G. Schirmer, Inc.

A thou- sand, thou- sand sweets ___ their fra- grant a - toms blend Which

In a _ gale of joy ___ which in a _ gale of joy ___ thy breath _____ at - tend, _ thy

Love in gen - tle mur - murs to my soul _____ ap - ply heal me with kiss- es Oh

heal ___ me _ with _ kiss- es or _ else _____ I _ die, _____ or _ else ___ I die.

(Play introduction as an ending.)

O DEL MIO AMATO BEN

Stephano Donaudy

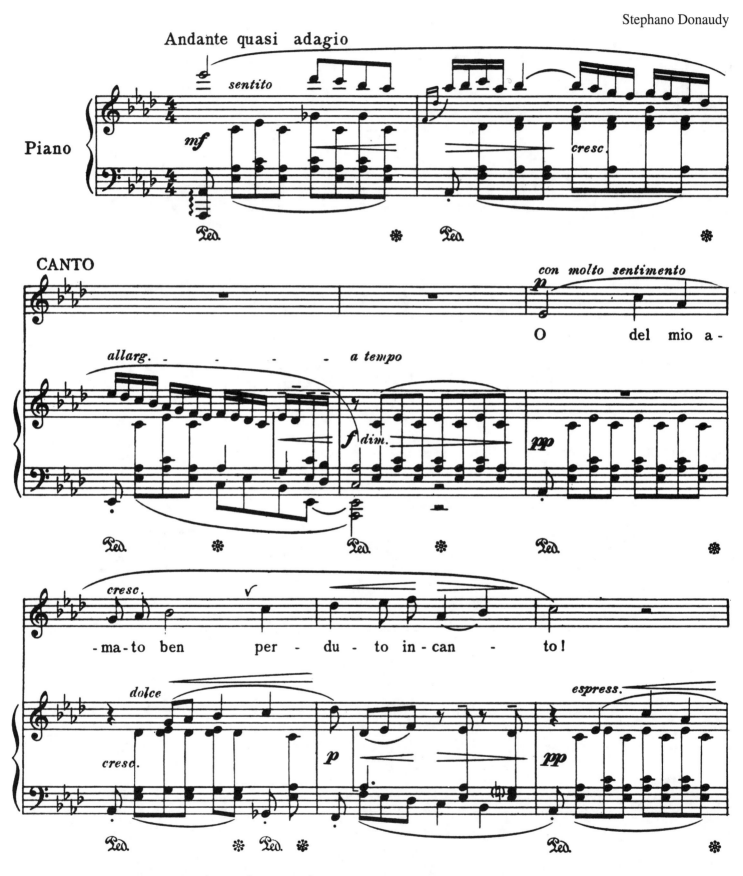

O del mio amato ben perduto incanto!   *O lost enchantment of my dear love!*

Printed in the USA by G. Schirmer, Inc.

Lungi è dagli occhi miei chi m'era gloria e vanto!   *Far from my sight is the one who was glory and pride to me!*

sem - pre la cer - co e chia - mo

con___ pie-no il cor___ di spe-ran - - ze Ma

cer - co in -van, chia-mo in-van! E il pian-ger m'è sì

Or per le mute stanze
sempre la cerco e chiamo
con pieno il cor di speranze...
Ma cerco invan, chiamo invan!

Now throughout the silent rooms
always I seek her and call out
with my heart full of hopes...
But I seek in vain; I call out in vain!

E il pianger m'è sì caro,
che di pianto sol nutro il cor.
Mi sembra, senza lei, triste ogni loco.

And weeping is so dear to me
that with weeping alone do I nourish my heart.
Without her, every place seems sad to me.

84

Notte me sembra il giorno;
mi sembra gelo il foco.
Se pur talvolta spero
di darmi ad altra cura,

Night seems like day to me;
fire seems ice-cold to me.
Even though at times I hope
to devote myself to another concern,

sol mi tormenta un pensiero:
ma, senza lei, che farò?
Mi par così la vita vana cosa
senza il mio ben.

a single thought torments me:
without her, what will I do?
Life like this seems a futile thing
without my beloved.
Translation by Martha Gerhart

ON RICHMOND HILL THERE LIVES A LASS

(The Lass of Richmond Hill)

James Hook

Allegretto

p
staccato

f

p

1. On Rich - mond Hill there lives a___ lass More
2. Ye Ze - phyrs gay that fan the air And
3. How hap - py will that shep - herd be Who

bright than May - day morn,_____ Whose charms all oth - er
wan - ton thro' the grove,_____ Oh whis - per to the
calls this nymph his own,_____ Oh may her choice be

Printed in the USA by G. Schirmer, Inc.

maids sur - pass, A rose with - out a thorn.
charm -ing fair I die for her I love.
fix'd on me; Mine's fix'd on her a - lone.

1. 2. 3. This lass so neat, with

smiles so sweet, Has won my right good will,_____ I'd

crowns re - sign to call thee mine, Sweet lass of Rich-mond

Hill! Sweet lass of Rich-mond Hill, Sweet

lass of Rich-mond Hill, _____ I'd crowns re-sign to

call thee mine, Sweet lass of Rich-mond Hill.

PANIS ANGELICUS
(O Lord Most Holy)

César Franck

O lov - ing Fa - ther, Thee would we be prais - ing
Dat pa - nis coe - li - cus fi - gu - ris ter - mi -

al - way. Help us to know_ Thee, know Thee and
num. O res mi - ra - bi - lis man - du - cat

love_ Thee; Fa - ther, Fa - ther, grant us Thy truth and
Do - mi - num, Pau - per, pau - per, ser - vus et hu - mi -

grace;   Fa - ther,   Fa - ther,   guide and de - fend___
lis,   *Pau - per,*   *pau - per,*   *(f) ser - vus et hu - mi -*

us.
lis.

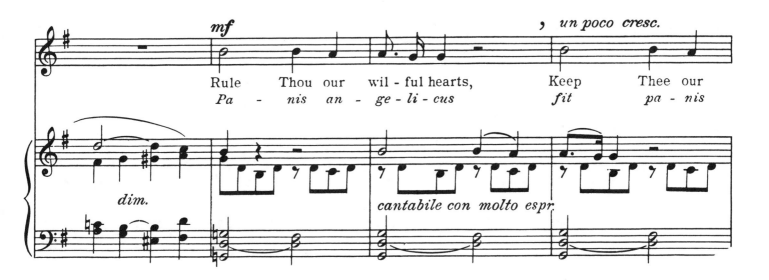

Rule   Thou our   wil - ful hearts,   Keep   Thee our
Pa - nis an - ge - li - cus   *fit*   *pa - nis*

In all our sorrows let us find our rest in
wan-d'ring thoughts;
ho - mi - num   (f) Dat   pa - nis   coe - li - cus   fi - gu - ris ter - mi -

Thee;   And   in temp - ta - tion's hour,   Save   through Thy
num,   O   res mi - ra - bi - lis   man - du - cat

might - y pow'r,   Thine   aid O send us;   Hear
Do - mi - num,   Pau - per, pau - per, ser -

us in mer - cy.   Show_____ us Thy

- vus et hu - mi - lis,   *Pau - - per,_*

fa - vor, So_____ shall we live, and sing praise____ to

pau - per, ser - vus,_ ser - vus et hu - mi -

Thee.

lis.

PHILLIS HAS SUCH CHARMING GRACES

Anthony Young
arranged by H. Lane Wilson

If __ not for __ me, __ not for me her __ ca - ress - es,

I ____ must __ love her though __ I _____ die.

Phil - lis has _____ such __ charm - ing grac - es, __

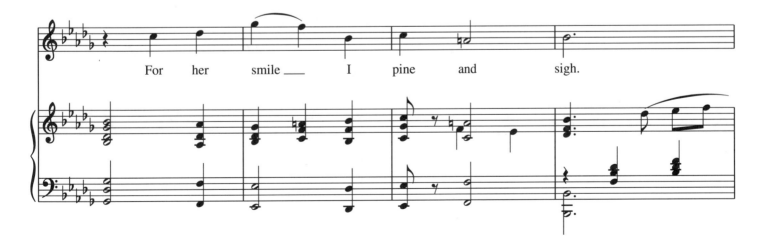

For her smile __ I pine and sigh.

accel. a poco

Love - ly __ Phil - lis, thou fair _____ de - stroy - er,

accel. a poco

Ease my trou - bled love - sick mind,

Smile _____ up - on _____ a hope - less _ lov - er,

Cease _____ to _ charm,, or else _____ be _____ kind.

Tempo I

Phil - lis has _____ such _ charm - ing grac - es, _____

I must love _____ her though _____ I die.

I _____ must love _ her though _ I die. _____

RUSSIAN PICNIC

Words and Music
(based on Russian Folk Tunes)
by Harvey Enders
(ASCAP)

The sun is high and bells are

ring - ing; _____ Young lads and maid - ens join in _____

cresc.

sing - ing; _____ Their songs and laugh - ter fill the

f accel.

air, A - cross the fields and vil - lage square. _____

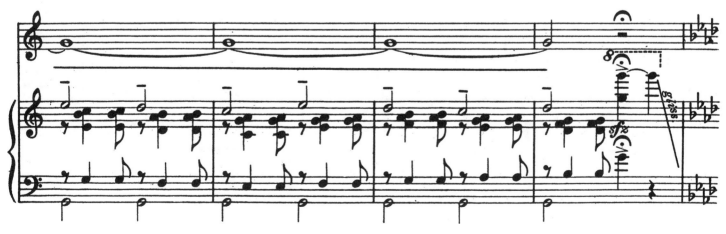

a tempo   *mf*

Play a tune, hey! hey! Ga - ran - ka;

Ba - la - lai - ka, strike! Ga - ran - ka; In and out with

old — *Gar - mosh - ka; Fin - gers danc - ing on — Gar - mosh - ka;

p cresc.

†Brin - da, brin - da, brin - da, brin - da, hey!   Brin - da, brin - da, brin - da, brin - da,

*A small accordion or concertina
† Brinda: No specific meaning; imitative of twanging strings, much like our "Plinkety Plunk"

hey! Ma-sha, Da-sha, Tan-ya, Ol-ga, Lift your feet and dance a pol-ka;

We'll make mer-ry all the day long On the banks of moth-er Vol-ga.

Soon the moon will rise up yon-der, Sil-ver moons make

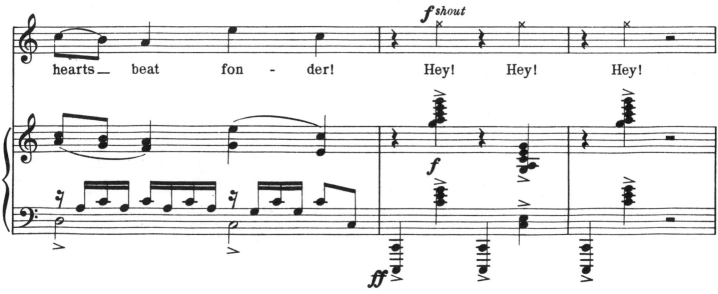

hearts beat fon - der! Hey! Hey! Hey!

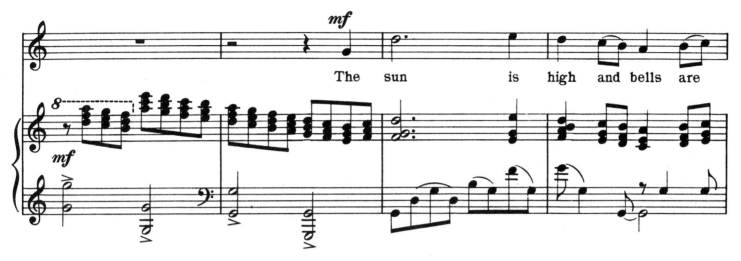

The sun is high and bells are

ring - ing; _____ Up - on the

breeze their songs are wing - ing; _____

Come, Ga - ran - - - - ka!

SEA FEVER

John Mansfield

John Ireland

all I ask is a wind _ y day with the white clouds fly _ ing, And the

flung spray and the blown spume, and the sea-gulls cry _ _ _ ing.

I must go down to the seas a _ gain, to the vag _ rant gyp _ sy life, To the

mf

p

pesante e cresc.

simile

gull's way and the whale's way, where the wind's like a whet-ted knife; And

all I ask is a mer-ry yarn from a laugh-ing fel-low-ro-ver, And

qui-et sleep and a sweet dream when the long trick's o - - - ver.

Chelsea: October 1913

STILLE SICHERHEIT

(Hark! How Still)

Nikolaus Lenau
translation by John S. Dwight

Robert Franz

SONNTAG
(Sunday)

Johann Ludwig Uhland
translation by Henry Chapman

Johannes Brahms

Op. 47, No. 3
Original key F major

woll - te Gott, woll - te Gott, ich wär' heu - te bei ihr!
Would to God, would to God I were with her to - day!

So will mir
And tho' in -

doch die gan - ze Wo - che das__ La - chen nicht ver - geh'n, ich sah
deed it's been a week now, I__ have not ceased to smile, For I

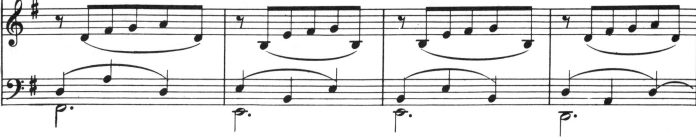

es an ei - nem Sonn - tag wohl in die Kir - che geh'n: das
gazed at her on Sun - day In__ church for such a while: My

tau - send-schö - ne Jung-fräu-lein, das tau - send-schö - ne Her - ze - lein,
rar - -est, fair - est lit - tle one, My neat - est, sweet -est pret - ty one:

woll - te Gott, woll - te Gott ich wär' heu - te bei ihr,
Would to God, would to God I were with her to - day!

woll - te Gott, woll - te Gott ich wär' heu - te bei ihr!
Would to God, would to God I were with her to - day!

WANDERERS NACHTLIED

(Wanderer's Night Song)

Johann Wolfgang von Goethe
translation by Theodore Baker

Franz Schubert

EL TROBADOR
(The Troubador)

Mexican Folksong
arranged by Edward Kilenyi

Yo tro - ba - dor, yo po - bre sin for - tu - na,
Poor trou - ba - dor am I, with for - tune frowning,

Si te ad - mi - ro, las gra - cias que tu tie - nes;
I love thee dear - ly, thy gra - ces I a - dore,

Yo no te veo, mas be - lla que la lu - na,
Like moon - light's spell thy beau - ty all is crown - ing,

Si te a - do - ro, me per - do - nas o - tra vez.
I love thee dear - ly. Oh! for - give___ me once more.

WEEP YOU NO MORE

Anonymous

Roger Quilter

waste! But my Sun's heav'n-ly eyes View not your

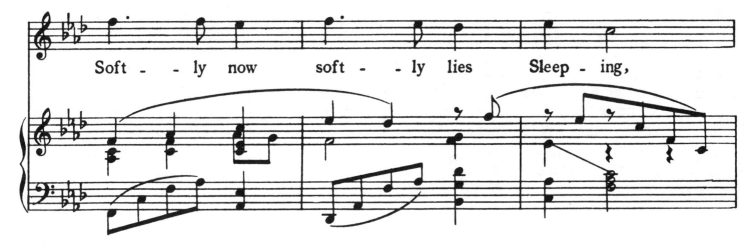

weep - ing, That now lies sleep - ing,

Soft - - ly now soft - ly lies Sleep - ing,

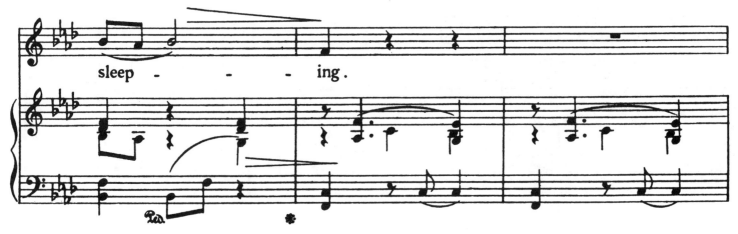

sleep - - - ing.

eyes! Melt not in weep - ing, While she lies

dolce.

sleep - ing, Soft - ly now soft - ly lies

Sleep - ing, sleep - - - ing.

WHERE'ER YOU WALK

from *Semele*

Edited by H. Heale

George Frideric Handel

trees, where you sit, shall crowd — in -

to — a shade.

Fine.

Wher - e'er · you tread, the blush-ing flow'rs shall rise, And

all things flour-ish, and all things flour-ish wher -

Adagio

e'er you turn your eyes, wher-e'er you turn your eyes, wher-e'er you turn your eyes.

D.C.

WHO IS SYLVIA?

William Shakespeare

Eric Coates

The heav'ns such grace did lend her, ... That she might ad-

-mir-ed be, ... That she might ad - mir - ed be.

Is she kind as she is fair? For beau - ty .....lives with kind - ness:

Is she kind as she is fair? For beau - ty ..... lives with kind - ness:

123

Love doth to her eyes re - pair, To help him of his blindness;

And, be - ing·help'd, in - hab - its there, in - ten

- hab - its there. Then to Syl - via

let us sing, That Syl - via is ex - cell - ing· Then to Syl - via

let us sing, That Syl - via is ex - cell - ing, She excels each

mor-tal thing Up - on the dull earth dwelling...............

To her let us gar-lands bring,...............

To her let us gar - lands bring...............

WHAT SONGS WERE SUNG

Words and Music by
John Jacob Niles

stood hard by While heav'n-ly sound filled up the sky.

Now let us stand, un-cov-ered all, Be-fore this crèche in low-ly stall, Where kings and an-gels dig-ni-fy God's gift, His Son, in hu-mil-i-ty.

We do not know, we can-not tell What

songs were sung, what_ star-light fell, Or why the ho-ly mys-ter-y stands For

so man-y years in so man-y lands. We

can-not tell, we do not know What stars shone down so_ long a-go, When

Mar-y birthed her own sweet Son And_ peace and love be-came as one.___